Roses

Contents

Contributors

Ai Kohno
Akari Inoguchi
Alexandra Compain-Tissier
Anna Higgie
Anne-Li Karlsson
Annika Wester
Asami Kiyokawa
Bela Borsodi
Camilla Dixon
Carine Brancowitz
Cecilia Carlstedt
Cedric Rivrain
Chinatsu Higashi
Christina K.
Coco Pit
David Despau
Elisa Johns
Esra Caroline Roise
Fifi Lapin
Géraldine Georges
Gi Myao
Helene Ryenbakken
Izumi Idoia Zubia
James Hamilton Butler
James Jean
Jarno Kettunen
Jeffrey Fulvimari
Julie Johnson
Kanako Sasaki

Karine Daisay
Kittozutto
Laura Laine
Little Thunder
Maki Kahori
Maren Esdar
Mat Maitland
Miyuki Ohashi
Nadia Flower
Naja Conrad-Hansen
Naoya Enomoto
Nori
Paula Sanz Caballero
Petra Dufkova
Raphaël Vicenzi
Ryo Sakuma
Sara D
Sayaka Hirota
Shinsuke Koshio
Tenna Hansen
Toshimitsu Haruka
Vincent Bakkum
Wendy Plovmand
Yoko Hasegawa
Yoshi Tajima
Yoshie
Ytje
ZAXIIV

Foreword

PERSIST EXPLORING THIS UNIQUE STYLE FROM AROUND THE WORLD AND NOW.

More than two years after the publication of The Age of Feminine Drawing, the art of the feminine continues to seduce us. But this time, we look beyond the decorative illustrations used to adorn fashionable products. This new edition pulls back the curtain to refocus the spotlight on the artists and the artwork itself.

The New Age of Feminine Drawing explores the process of creation behind the scenes, exposing the work that results in a holistic embodiment of feminine style and subjectivity.

While feminine drawing has always been hard to define, it is hardly limited to illustration. Collecting inspirational elements from a variety of sources, developing the artwork into a multimedia palette, today's feminine drawing is more about form than content.

Many artists begin with what they can touch — picking up stray materials, scanning in sketches, choosing from a database of visual elements — before fusing them all into a digital collage.

"For a fashion illustration, I generally start by sketching out the pose and then scanning it in and cleaning it in Photoshop," says Cecilia Carlstedt.

Laura Laine

"I like to keep the tone of the paper to have the feeling of an original. Then I color in some parts and maybe bring in a pattern that I have created in Illustrator or scan in an ink-blob that could be used as texture. It's in Photoshop that I put all the elements together. In the end, the image becomes sort of a collage of different techniques, textures and styles."

This book features the work of artists who incorporate drawings, watercolors, painting, photography, textiles, strings and other found objects into a mixed-media palette of what finally emerges as a feminine creation.

Of course, the word "feminine" itself is no less loaded, always open to interpretation and often the source of provocative variation.

Jarno Kettunen

Cecilia Carlstedt

WHAT IS "FEMININE"?

One of the few male artists featured in this book, Vincent Bakkum, recalls witnessing a street rally against a female beauty pageant in India. One of the women's banners read: "Stop objectifying us!"

"The slogan distracts and haunts me," says Vincent. "I also objectify the female by painting her the way I like to see her (in my paintings): slender, bony almost, lightly dressed and with an often arrogant stare. Somehow my esthetics are part of the egocentric, inconsiderate realm of media and advertising... While I represent female beauty, I feel constantly scrutinized by women with red dots between their eyes."

Nonetheless, Vincent celebrates the "transcendent beauty of a certain type of woman" just as much as he enjoys painting "exotic, colorful birds".

Another male artist, Cédric Rivrain, simply describes femininity as "sensitivity, intensity, sensuality, beauty".

Meanwhile many female artists embrace conventional views of femininity by exploring its various forms in their own work.

"Feminine for me is a world of grace," says Alexandra Compain-Tissier. "Sexy attitudes, soft colors, bright pink, strawberry, tenderness, details and round shape, nice fragrance, embroidery and jewelry."

"Feminine is a set of ideas, clichés, that I like to play with," says Anne-Li Karlsson. "The stereotype is one starting point for my work. I use them and abuse them the way I want, and in the end, hopefully I complicate the cliché and make it less perfect, more human and fun."

Other artists highlight the feminine by contrasting it with impressions of the masculine.

For Camilla Dixon, "Femininity is the natural unconscious expression of female shape, movement and aura. [But] it is most stunning when emphasized by the contrast of a slightly masculine presentation: clean lines, a boyish cut, and no frills!"

"'Feminine' characterizes the female spirit or relates to the female identity in our society," confirms Bela Borsodi. "It also means to be the opposite of 'masculine', and both these terms need each other to exist; they are in a direct connection. Best is if these are in a good, inspiring balance."

Top: YOSHIE
Bottom: Vincent Bakkum

Curiously, Carine Brancowitz cites the actress Anouk Aimée in the classic 1966 French film "A Man and a Woman".

Still more intriguing are the interpretations of several Japanese artists, for whom the feminine concept evokes elusive, irrational associations.

Among Chinatsu Higashi's visual associations are "ribbon in a bow, Jane Birkin, Kubrick's Lolita, Sofia Coppola's movies, my mom," but who would have guessed "pigeon-toed people"?

And perhaps most enigmatic is Yoshi Tajima's concise portrait of the "girl with the loneliest eyes".

But just as we are reminded that the medium is the message, so are we all the more fascinated by the process behind the product.

So we invite you to share our glimpse into these artists' imaginations through their real-world studios, as they experiment with matter over mind in this new age of feminine drawing.

Naja Conrad-Hansen

I think softness is feminine.

At the moment I'm really into drawing twisted-bodied girls with a melancholy attitude. I start with an idea of what feeling and movement I want the end result to have, and then as I draw the idea develops and gets more defined. I draw with pencil and markers and finally retouch the image in Photoshop.

—— *Laura Laine*

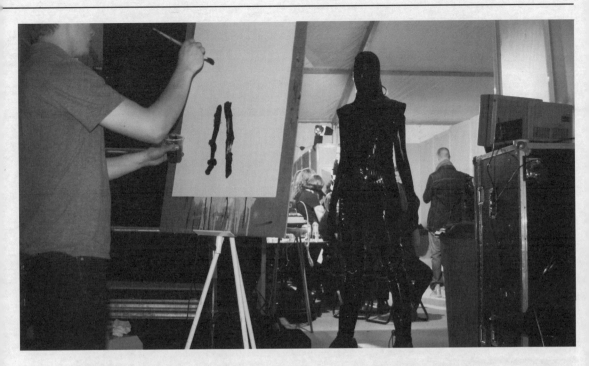

For me feminine means sensual,
emotional, compassionate and subtle.

In my work I try to approach and describe feminine themes in my own way – as a man who admires and is fascinated by the feminine side of things. I am more interested in expressing attitude, emotions and feelings in my drawings than the actual reality. My pictures are challenging, but that's the way I want them to be.

—— *Jarno Kettunen*

Feminine is pink.
I feel it is a very emotional color.

My work expresses an organic sensuality I feel is peculiar to women.
It also shows esthetic derived from my nostalgia for my own
Japanese culture.

—— *Akari Inoguchi*

Feminine is soft, alluring, deceptively powerful, sexual.

My work is a culmination of things that attract me in both a beautiful and a repulsive way. The work focuses on the glamorous, the natural, and the absurd.

—— *Elisa Johns*

Feminine for me is many things,
but the first I think is details in a work
and a great eye for color.

Many more men than women are color-blind. I'm obsessed with fairy tales,
fantasy and day dreaming. I'd like it to have a playful feeling and not take
itself too seriously, which I think is probably a reflection of myself.

—— *Naja Conrad-Hansen*

In my eyes feminine drawing represents enchanting, delicate, glamorous, sometimes poetic, fleeting...

My work is the achievement of a long research, a composition of a lot of ideas and inspirations. I'm very interested in fashion, so my drawings are essentially figurative themes, for example fashion design or impression, but I make graphic works, prints and color-intensive paintings and textile paintings too.

—— *Petra Dufkova*

My work communicates my inspirations, knowledge, feelings ...

Tenderness. I think feminine is feeling all things around myself. Feminine is like pastel-colored acrylic, it gives us a soft and tender feeling. When I am sad, make others laugh. When I am happy, spread it to others. Think about other people and make them smile, I think this is feminine.

—— *Yoshie*

Feminine is pale flaky walls and prominent collar bones, the waving of silk and the African sand dunes.

My work is poetic, ethereal, dainty. Any pale color in combination with strong fluorescent ones can break my heart.

—— *Christina K.*

"My" women are feminine, extremely feminine.

My every painting is a small personal victory over death. I'm desperately stealing beauty from it.

—— Vincent Bakkum

I consider harmony, softness, sensitiveness, emotional wisdom, lavishness, elegance and allurement to be "feminine".

If I had to choose a color, I'd pick purple and all its different shades! I think my work is really rather feminine, for I consider it to be poetic, smooth, elegant and full of harmony - there's no harshness or aggressivity, no loud colors.

—— Maren Esdar

Feminine is powerful without a doubt.

I definitely think pink, peach and violet are feminine colors. When my work is colorful, it is pretty, and in black and white, it often has more attitude.

—— *Annika Wester*

Feminine is silk.

*My work is intuitive, experimental
and essentially linked to the world of fashion.*

—— *Cecilia Carlstedt*

While feminine drawing has always been hard to define, it is hardly limited to illustration. Collecting inspirational elements from a variety of sources, developing the artwork into a multimedia palette, today's feminine drawing is more about form than content...

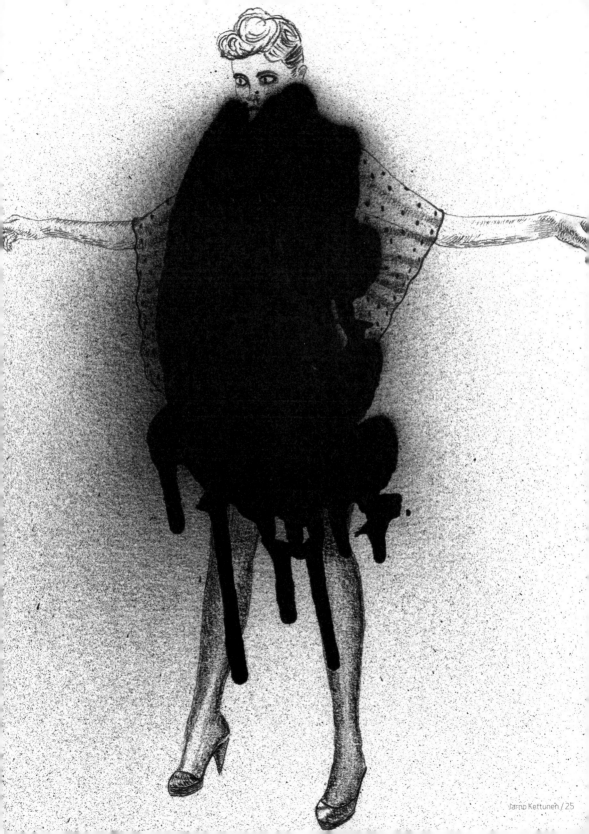

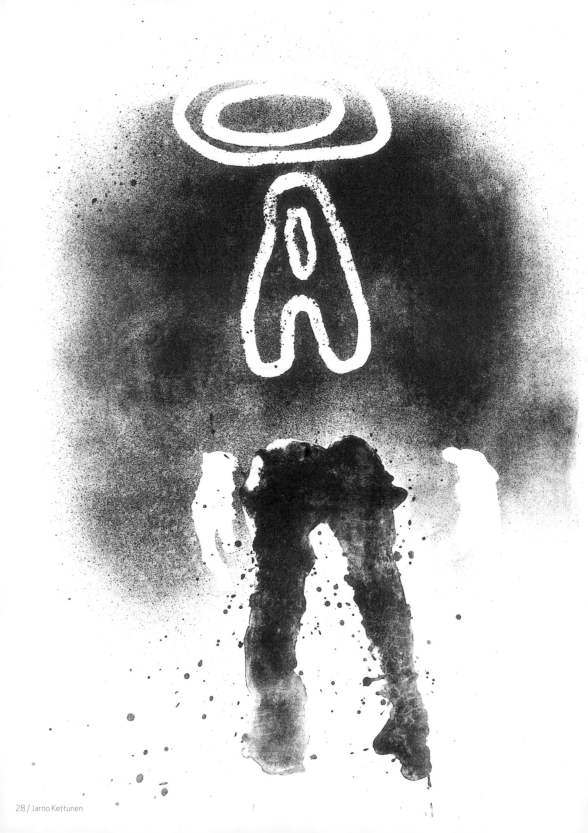

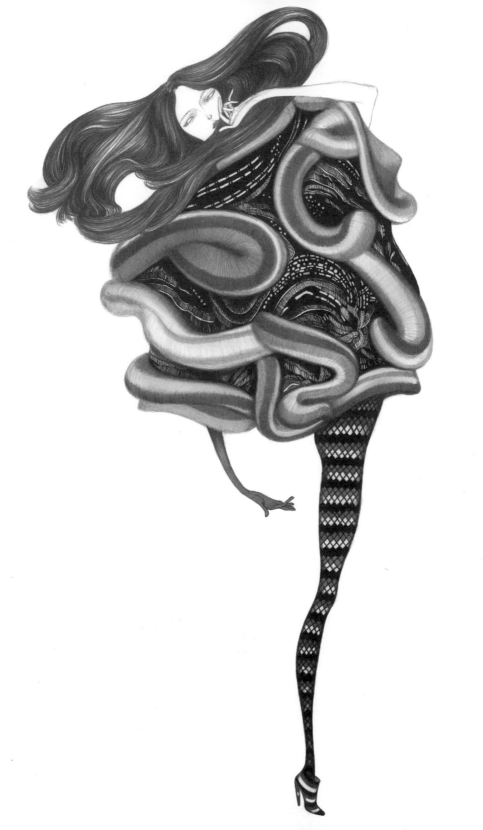

THINGS ARE COOL

a girl with a bowler hat

DEMURE
UNTAMED

ALEXIS MABILLE   ANNA VINCE
FLORIAN   HOUSE OF FLORA
HUSAM EL ODEH JOHANNE MILLS
SCOTT STEPHEN   SCOTT WILSON

HAPPY NEW YEAR

NEW YEAR - NEW WEBSITE
WWW.ANTIMONIDE.COM

VALERY DEMURE
PRESENTS...

\\ HOUSE OF FLORA, MISS BIBI,
PHILIPPE ROUCOU

THE ECONOMY

i had to leave town because of a fashion mistake

dynasty

Tenna Hansen / 93

DETAILS - "DRAWN TOGETHER" - USA 2006

ELLE - "ALTO PROFILO" - ITALY 2008

interview with **BELA BORSODI**

FROM BEAUTY TO PHOTO

"I want to challenge the obvious function and position of things to eventually find a new possible context and meaning for them. I want to share my enthusiasm and communicate my experiences. I also want to make this process visible and to do so playfully."

—— *Bela Borsodi*

What is "feminine" in your eyes?

"Feminine" characterizes the female spirit or relates to the female identity in our society. It also means to be the opposite of "masculine". Both these terms need each other to exist, as they are in a direct connection. Best is if they are in a good, inspiring balance. Because I am a man, the term "feminine" could either describe something that is "different" from me or it could also describe something "other", that I might desire or that I have fantasies about. I personally don't have too many thoughts on this, because I believe that my masculinity early on was also in touch with my "feminine" qualities. Feminine qualities are nothing really alien to me, and they don't "threaten" my masculinity.

How do you describe your work?

My work is a visual investigation of perception and I use photography for this process. I want to challenge the obvious function and position of things to eventually find a new possible context and meaning for them. I want to share my enthusiasm and communicate my experiences. I also want to make this process visible and to do so playfully.

How would your life be divided up on a daily basis between all activities, ranging from sleep to working to creative activities?

It is really impossible for me to even imagine of how to divide up my interests and activities. My life is all about the exact opposite: that everything comes together and is directly connected; that all happens simultaneously.

What would you usually do to grasp inspirations?

Imagine things which do not exist already. Use my curiosity to explore things and go on adventures. I am, of course, also very easily inspired by many different things around me (art, movies, stories, etc, as well as "life" itself), but I believe that true inspiration is something that makes me investigate things that are new to me. I usually take my notebook and draw, or I close my eyes and imagine things and let them take me places.

Your images are composed of fashion items, graphics and sometimes even papercuttings. When did you first become interested in making these kinds of images to present your ideas?
To work with fashion items is just a way for me to explore my ideas and to find a place for my projects. I choose the materials or graphic elements in my images according to their quality for each project. When I was a kid I was always drawing and building things, and that has never changed. For me it is the most natural thing to constantly get my fingers onto materials and to explore them and to play. Every project is an adventure to me, and I am lucky that I can make this my profession.

How are fashion photography, graphics and papercuttings related within each image?
Every element is necessary for the other to exist, and together they all make up the image. It is a playful process to watch them take shape and interact with each other; very often some elements take on a particular and unexpected character, which can challenge the entire project. I love when this happens, because I believe that only in an actual process can one find out more about the true nature of one's project. The discipline of an artist is to learn to respect the lively and independent personality of his own creation, so that the creation can enter into a dialogue with its creator.

Which creator has influenced you most?
To not just mention the more obvious, I want to name here Jean-Luc Godard. His work challenged established structures, and he created a new identity and a new syntax of film. He re-evaluated a conventional perception and questioned the essence of film. He established a new and fresh reality of what film can be, and he brought in other elements and ideas from different disciplines: art, philosophy, literature, history, politics, advertising, music, mythology, etc. He put these into juxtaposition and dialogue. Thus he changed the reality and the syntax of film, and he also created a new esthetic — visual, narrative and conceptual. I find his work very inspiring — to rethink all that is familiar to me and to explore obvious structures in order to find a different approach.

Making-of "ALTO PROFILO"

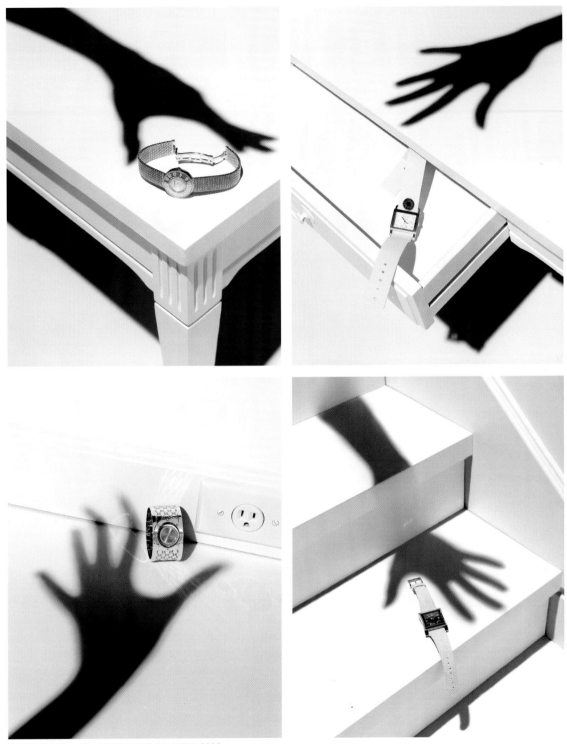

VOGUE NIPPON #83 - "STEALING TIME" - JAPAN 2006

For your work in Stern #36, "Aus Dem Shatten Getreten", you use ladies' shoes and accessories to sculpt a female figure. What are the ideas and process behind these images?

That story is conceptual, actually quite different from how you describe it. I did not shape the female figure out of product, rather I placed product into the opening of a white wall. These openings had the shape of female figures. These 'figures' did not even actually exist, because in reality they are only empty space. These shapes illustrate the missing woman who would wear or desire these products. While she is 'absent', only the product is 'present'.

This was one of my most favorite projects, and it went through many stages of conceptualizing before it all fit together. It was quite difficult to develop these female shapes, because to create an attractive and functional silhouette takes a lot of consideration. After I had designed these figures I flew to Paris, then the sets were built there, and the products were placed into the figures.

Making-of "AUS DEM SCHATTEN GETRETEN"

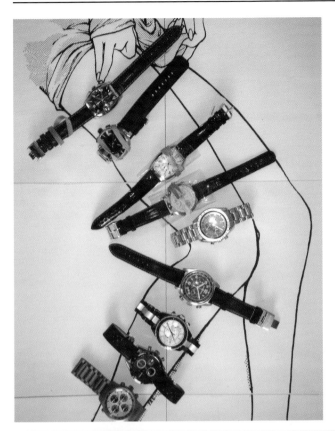

Bela Borsodi
Born in Vienna, Austria, in 1966. Based in New York City. Borsodi specializes in still-life photography as he toys with human perception, combining unexpected elements with fashion, styling and set design.

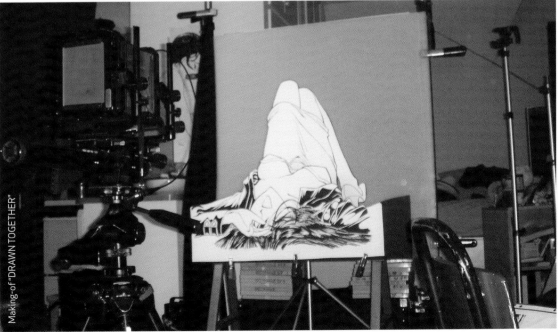

Making-of "DRAWN TOGETHER"

FROM DRAWING TO FASHION

"I like pen and ink,
because I fell in love with the smell of India ink in high school.
It's a nostalgic reason."

—— *Jeffrey Fulvimari*

How would your life be divided up on a daily basis between all activities, ranging from sleep to creative pursuits?
It varies from day to day. When I have a deadline, I sometimes work all day, and only sleep and eat after the job is done.

How do you describe your work?
I am a commercial illustrator. I use pen and ink, and also computer.

How did you first become interested in this style of drawing?
I developed this style because in the beginning, it was easy to get jobs. I only used black pen line at the time, and people hired me because they didn't have to have a large budget and many colors at the time.

What is "feminine" in your eyes?
Well, also when I started drawing, I drew many different things. I actually started out doing caricatures. But over time people really responded to my drawings of girls, and they became most popular. But the concept of "feminine" is really too wide a subject to put into words. I think femininity is a subject matter that goes back very far in history.

What is the process for developing and finishing a drawing?
I start with the eyes, and then fill everything else in around them.

What do you usually do for inspiration?
I like to look at pictures on the internet. Sometimes for backgrounds, or just a feeling. Most of the time the finished product has little to do with the reference photo.

Which creator has influenced you most?
Charles Shultz, creator of Peanuts. I love the way he uses the least amount of lines to depict something.

What are your favorite color and drawing media?

My favorite color changes all the time. Right now it is probably green, because it's a color I didn't like for the longest time. I like pen and ink, because I fell in love with the smell of India ink in high school. It's a nostalgic reason.

Which one of your past works do you like the most?

Of mine...I really like an invitation I did for a charity event in NYC that depicted a medieval theme. I actually like to draw fantasy themes more than contemporary ones. I loved illustrators from the 1920s and '30s, and they usually did fantasy themes.

What are you working on now?

Right now I am working on the English Roses chapter books. We have published 11 of them in the States, and there is one more to go in the series, which makes 12.

What are you interested in recently?

I am starting to become interested in doing completely different subject matter or themes than what I am known for, as a sideline and a diversion.

Jeffrey Fulvimari

Born in Akron, Ohio. Fulvimari started his illustration career in 1993, working on commissions for Barney's New York and Interview magazine. Since 1999, Jeffrey has helped produce licensed goods in Japan, and has launched product lines in the US, UK, France, Italy and Mexico.

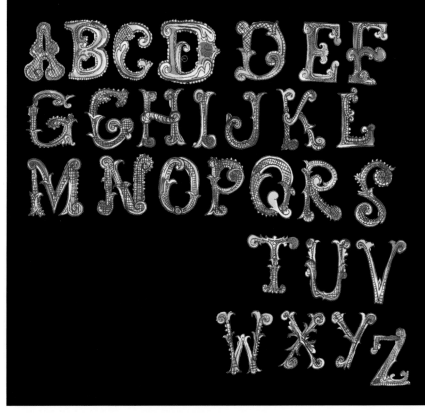

please buy my record.
Candy put 2 years of heartache and personal growth into one compact disc...

FROM SKETCH TO FABRIC

*"For me feminine is tenderness,
feeling all things around myself, pastel-color acrylics…"*

—— *Yoshie*

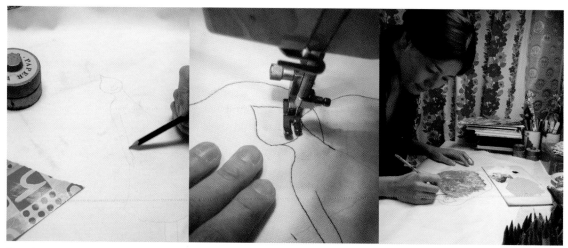

Sketch

Think of an image and draw it on the cloth. With a sewing machine, stitch over the lines of the drawing.

Paint

Use acrylics to paint hair.

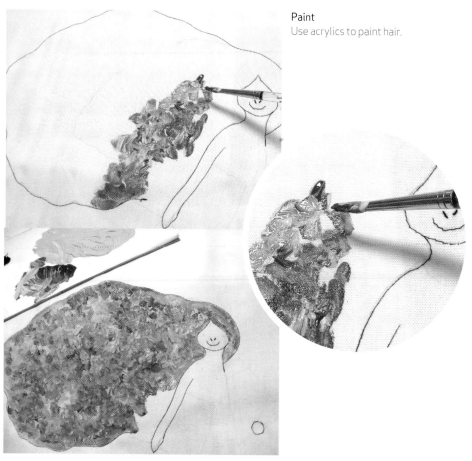

Match with fabric

Once you have the hair, put many pieces of fabric on the drawing, and repeat until you find what pleases you. Add eyes, cheeks, beads, ribbons, etc, and finish! This is Yoshie's "Fabric-Illustration".

How would you describe your work?
I communicate my inspirations, knowledge, feelings, etc, through my creations.

How did you first become interested in this style of illustration?
I always enjoy picking up random fabrics, colorful paints, and intuitively combining them. I went to fashion school, so fabrics have naturally become part of my artwork.

What is "feminine" in your eyes?
Tenderness. I think feminine is feeling all things around myself. Feminine is like pastel-color acrylics. (They give us a soft and tender feeling.) Busy and sad, but instead of my sadness, I make others laugh. When I am happy, I share my happiness with others. Thinking about making other people smile, this is feminine.

What is the process for developing and finishing a drawing?
I start with a rough image, then go from there. The colors come naturally, so I don't really plan the path.

What do you usually do for inspiration?
Go for a walk, meet friends, meet new people and sometimes even go abroad.

Which creator has influenced you most?
Edgar Degas, I love everything about his works. But my primary influence would be my grandmother, who created everything by hand.

What are your favorite color and drawing media?
I love using fabrics, acrylic paints, stitching, etc. I don't have any preferences concerning color, as I love all colors.

Which one of your past works do you like the most?
All! I can't pick only ONE of them!

What are you working on now?
Recently I've been creating pictures for magazines, advertisements, CD jackets, etc, in Japan. I've also held exhibitions for my works, such as picture story books.

What are you interested in recently?
Traveling, music, as well as belly dancing! I'd like to experience colors, fabrics, lifestyle and cultures from around the world.

Yoshie (Yoshie Uchimura)
Based in Tokyo. Yoshie has been working as an illustrator since 2005, creating artworks on cloth or paper using scraps of fabrics, stitching, acrylic, collage, etc. Besides working for art exhibitions, she also teaches collage workshops for adults and children. She has published picture books in Japan, including "Yoshie-Fondre", "Ponpor-tontan" and "TSUKIMIMOZA".

..... brought us to the POLKA THEATRE FOR CHILDREN Ages 0 - 13 !!

♪ Wimbledom ♪ Tennis ♪

LOVELY POP-UP cards

€ 4⁵⁰ ~

at Mr, Steve's Corner

interview with **MAKI KAHORI**

FROM PENCIL TO FANTASY

"I live in my fantasy world. I draw by pencil on paper first, then scan it, then compose on a computer. I like black, green, pink, because they are beautiful colors. I also like watercolor ink and pencil, because they excite me."

—— *Maki Kahori*

I use a pencil from 4H to 6B, sharp pencil 0.5 and 0.3, from 2H to 4B. I stock them separately.

Step 1 : I use a sample photo that I took myself, or sometimes pick one from the internet.
2B pencil for the first step.
Step 2 : 6B for dark parts, 4H for light parts.
Step 3 : Fine parts using 0.3 sharp pencil. It takes so much time for one flower...
Step 4 : A printing company scans my drawing, then I cut it on the computer.
Step 5-7 : Then I compose everything on the computer — Photoshop CS3.
Step 8 : Finished.

Maki Kahori
Born in 1969. After graduating from the Art Department of Japan University in 1992, she lived in New York for two years before returning to Tokyo. Her first solo exhibition, "Song from NY", was held at Gallery House Maya in Aoyama. Maki now works as a freelance illustrator for magazines and advertising, while doing her own artwork and often contributing to performing arts. She also published a book: "18 Art Street".

How would your life be divided up on a daily basis between all activities, ranging from sleep to creative pursuits?
40% painting, drawing by hand/computer 30% e-mail, transportation, free time, etc. 30% sleep

How do you describe your work?
I am living in my fantasy world.

When did you first become interested in this drawing style?
In 2005, I just wanted to draw in a different style from what I had done before.

What is "feminine" in your eyes?
A curved line.

What is the process for developing and finishing a drawing?
I draw by pencil on paper first, then a printer scans it, then I compose the image on a computer.

What do you usually do for inspiration?
Walk in nature.

Which creator has influenced you most?
The artist Tomoko Konoike.

What are your favorite color and drawing media?
Black, green, pink... they are beautiful. Watercolor ink, pencil... because they excite me.

Which one of your past works do you like the most?
CD jacket: HIATUS
I have done the work before I have noticed(without known).

What are you working on now?
As an artist, I'm preparing for next competition and exhibition. As an illustrator, I'm drawing for posters and packaging in the fashion & beauty world.

What are you interested in recently?
Breath.

Photograph by Yoshitsugu Enomoto

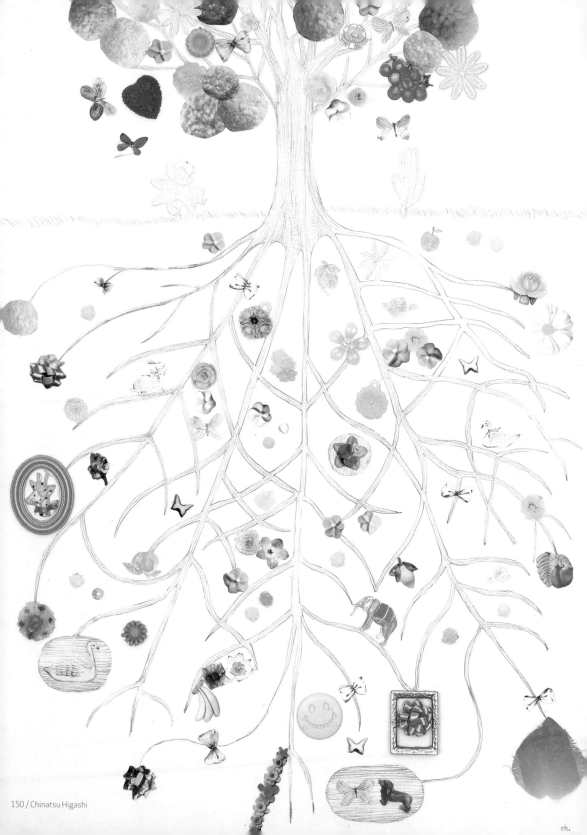

PARCO SWIM DRESS

夏盛り❤

PARCO
www.parco-swim.com

modi
summer

modi
spring

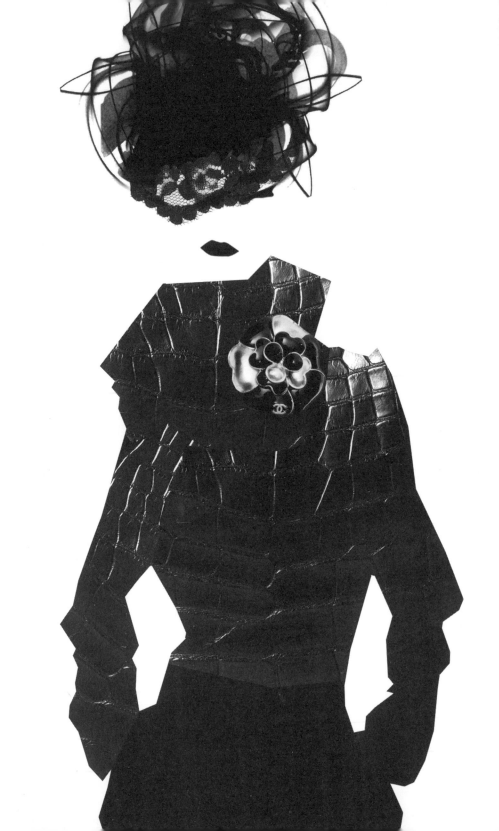

Miyu

magazine「Milk Japon」"milk drop"/X-Knowledge/no.4/200

Mêtr

MIYU

ROMANTIC BLOUSE

GIVENCHY ON 5
YIGAL AZROUEL ON 5
JEAN PAUL GAULTIER ON 5
SHOES ON 5

MasterCard

CHARMED, WE'RE SURE

WITH A HIGHLY ACCLAIMED ALBUM AND MORE MOVIE ROLES THAN EVER— NOT TO MENTION HER UNIQUELY ENDEARING BRAND OF QUIRKINESS— **ZOOEY DESCHANEL** IS THE ULTIMATE IT GIRL.

BY APRIL LONG.
PHOTOGRAPHED BY HILARY WALSH

CHRISTINE YUEON

PHOTOGRAPHY **MARIANO VIVANCO**
STYLING **NICOLA FORMICHETTI**

122 DAZED & CONFUSED

CHRISTINE YAFON

PHOTOGRAPHY **MARIANO VIVANCO**
STYLING **NICOLA FORMICHETTI**

122 DAZED & CONFUSED

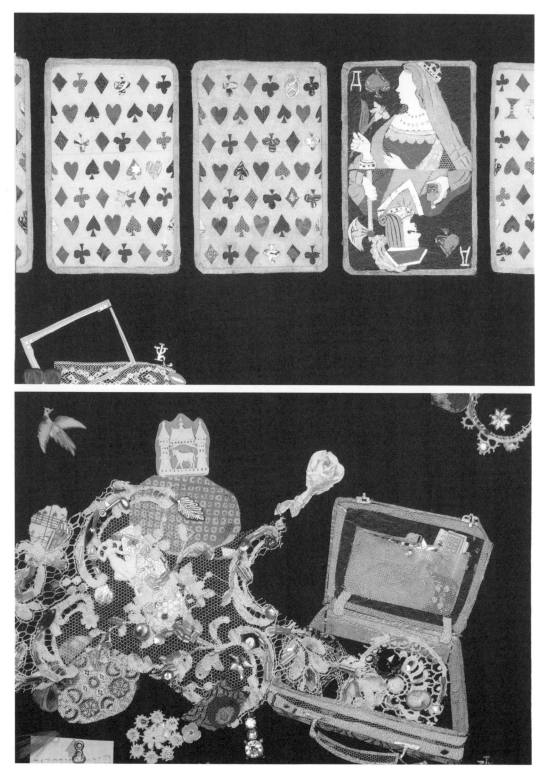

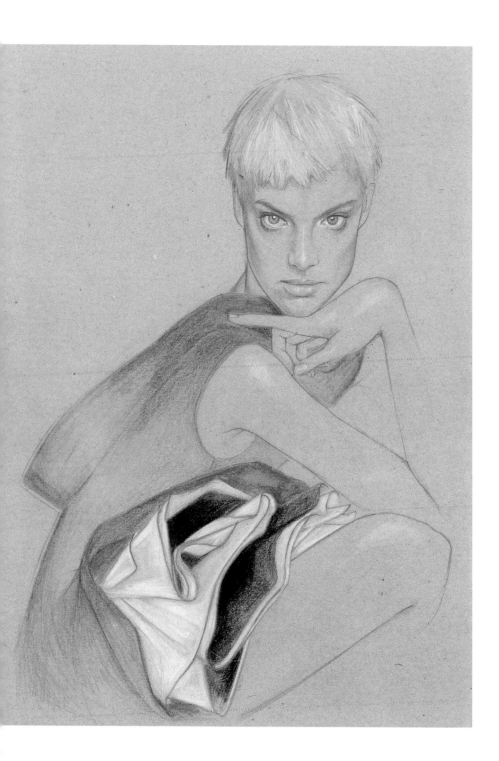

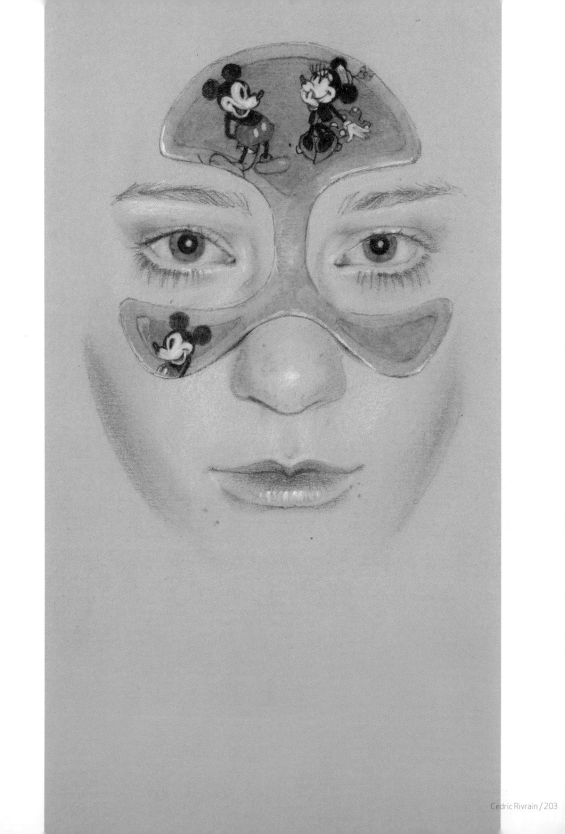

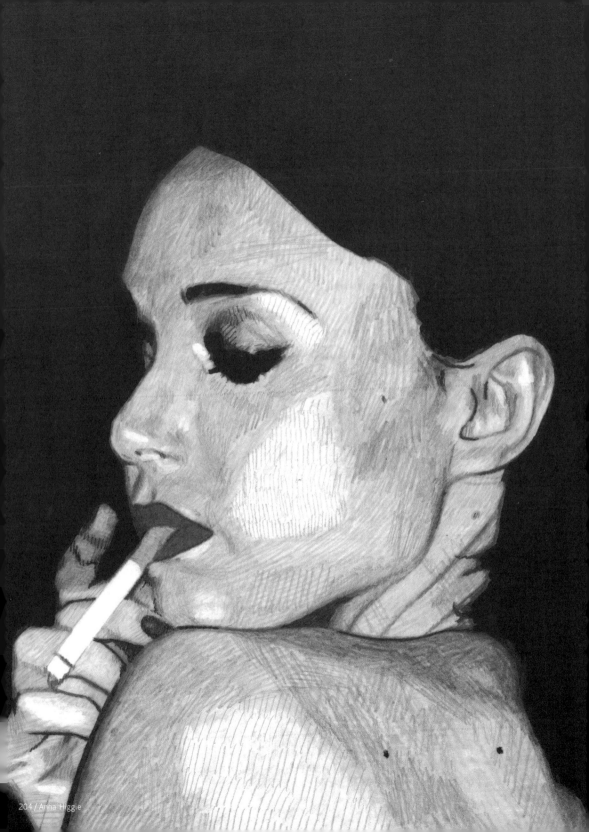

Loser

Kanako Sasaki / 241

Johnson

Cédric Rivrain / 249

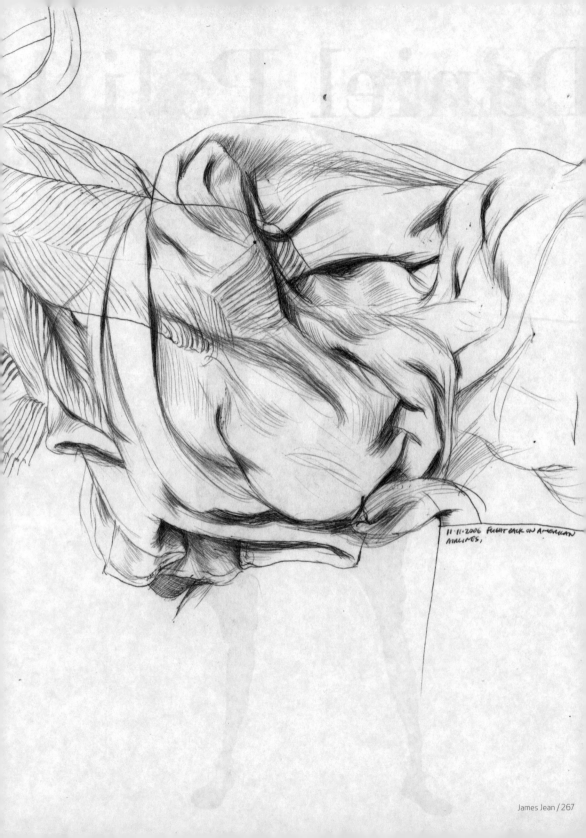

11·11·2006 FLIGHT BACK ON AMERICAN AIRLINES,

Daniel Palillo

Laura Laine / 269

Tenna Hansen / 271

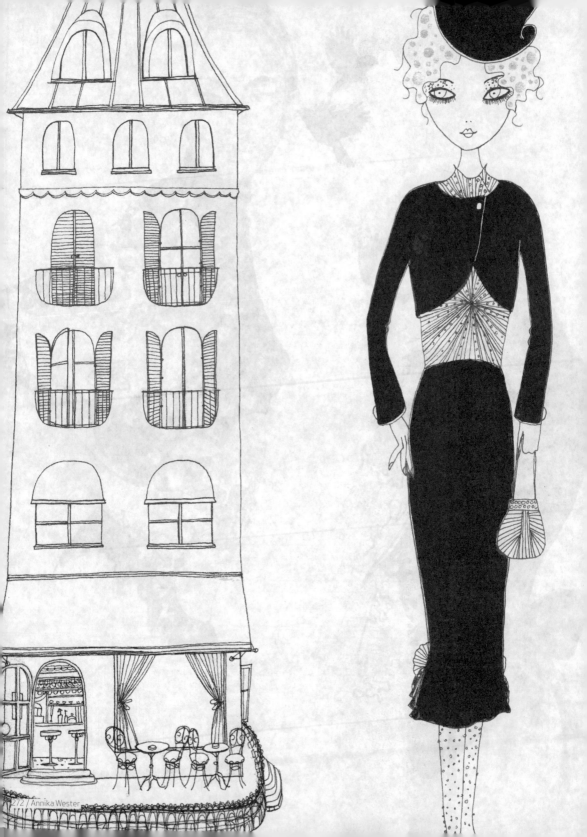

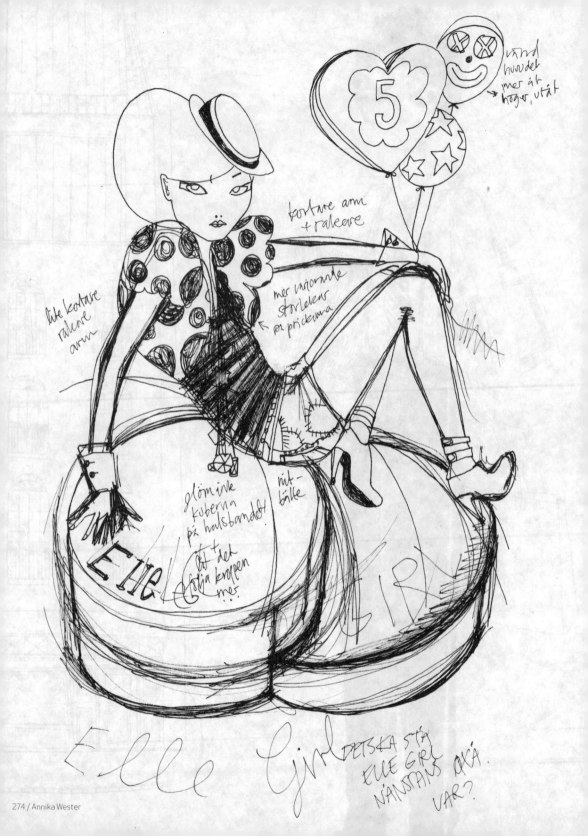

GOLD

BLACK

Behind the scenes

Taking a peek inside the artist's studio gives an exclusive insight into the artwork, examining the cradle of creation and discovering the process behind the product. Here the artists have generously pulled back the curtain to reveal the intimacy of their personal workspaces, inviting us to imagine further how environment influences artistry

AI KOHNO

"I express light and motion through dots and lines in the monochromatic world. I wish for the audience to imagine or feel a story behind every creature that appears in my drawings."

Japan | Illustrator

Born in Chiba, Japan, in 1984. Based in Tokyo. Ai Kohno had dreamed of being an illustrator since childhood. Finally in 2007, she quit her job in an advertising company to follow her dream. Her first professional illustrations were mainly composed of lines and dots in a monochromatic tone, used as apparel graphics in magazines, catalogues, retail displays, fashion shows, as well as exhibitions.

My favorite color is pink. I feel it is a very feminine and emotional color.

AKARI INOGUCHI

"I was drawing pictures of girls ever since I can remember. Maybe I was influenced by Japanese girls' comic books. My biggest influence is Takashi Murakami. He was the first Japanese artist to become successful in the Western fine-art market. I feel that he created a new platform, opening the way for young Japanese artists. I also feel very close to his philosophy of merging high art and low art."

Japan | Illustrator, designer

Born in Hokkaido in 1984. Graphic designer and visual artist working in a diverse range of media. She contributes illustrations to fashion magazines, television commercials, product packaging and labels, t-shirts and textile designs. Akari also produces paintings, drawings, digital prints and murals, and has participated in numerous shows in the U.S. and Japan.

I like painting both on paper and in Photoshop. I go back and forth between analogue and digital formats as much as necessary until I can create a unique integration.

ALEXANDRA COMPAIN-TISSIER

"My work is realistic and feminine, it's a mix of a classic technique with contemporary subjects and colorful images. Step 1: I get inspired by someone or something. Step 2: I do pictures or research on the Internet. Step 3: I do a collage then a sketch in black and white with simple lines. Step 4: I paint or I draw, it depends on the subject. Step 5: I do a scan on my computer and sometimes I change a few details in Photoshop."

France | Painter & illustrator

Born in Versailles, France, in 1971. Graduated from the Higher National School of Plastic Arts in Cergy. Working from photographs and collages, Alexandra draws in black and white and watercolors. Her first collection of drawings, "Dumbo Alex", was published by Flux. She made an animated music video for the band TTC at Ninja Tune, and has sold illustrations for both private collections and international stores and magazines.

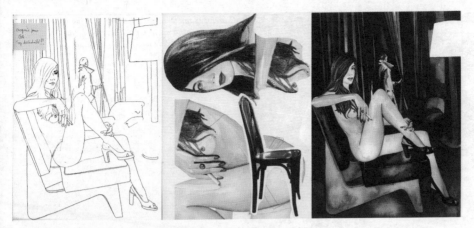

Before using watercolors, I was doing pencil drawings. But I realized that I was missing the dimension of color, so six years ago I decided to paint with watercolor, because it gives bright light and colors.

Currently I divide my time between working with clients, pursuing my own projects and teaching, all of which feed off each other, so it's quite inspiring. It's an ecosystem of my own.

ANNE-LI KARLSSON

"I usually start with an idea, a feeling and a composition, and then I sketch myself towards that. On the way, I often use friends or myself as a model when I need to see how a hand, for instance, actually looks at a certain angle. The final touch is usually made on the computer."

Sweden | Illustrator

Born in Seoul, South Korea, and raised in Stockholm, Sweden. Graduated with a Bachelor of Graphic Design and Illustration at Konstfack, Stockholm, and a Master of Design at California College of the Arts in San Francisco in 2004. She now works in Stockholm as an illustrator for graphic design, motion graphics and animation, as well as live wall painting and personal exhibitions.

ANNIKA WESTER

"My works changed a great deal after I moved to Paris from Sweden in 2005 to find inspiration for my own, non-commissioned work. I became more of a fashion illustrator, while drawing in a place where fashion is taken more seriously. Also Paris is a very beautiful city to live in, which helps."

France | Illustrator

Based in Paris. While growing up in Sweden, Annika made thin-line drawings with ink pen after gazing through hundreds of comics. She later studied at the Hungarian Academy of Fine Arts in Budapest. The fashionable girls in her illustrations combine innocent allure and vintage style. In 2005, her illustrations of fashion accessories were featured in a solo show titled "Portraits of Girls" at Gallery Lele in Tokyo.

My process for developing and finishing a drawing is just to start, then to forget everything else around me so as to be focused enough to finish.

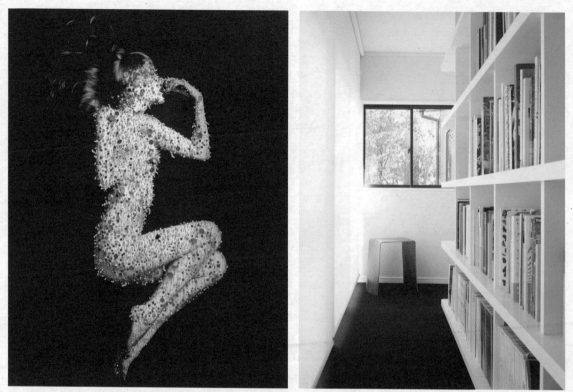

My artwork "Complex-skin", 2008

ASAMI KIYOKAWA

"In my eyes, feminine is sexy. My work is delicate, with impact. When I first wanted to draw, I had only some strings. But strings have various expressions. Now I make textiles, take photos, then do embroidery on the photos."

Japan | Art director

Born in Hyogo, Japan, in 1979. Asami makes fiber and textile art, clothing, art spaces, films and illustrations. She also does art direction for CD jackets and advertisements. She was behind the creative direction, fashion design and artwork of the 2007 publication "Asami Kiyokawa catch the girl", a collection of photography featuring famous actresses, celebrities and musicians posed as flora and fauna.

My studio (photo by Daici Ano)

CAMILLA DIXON

"The infinite wealth of possibilities available through collage make it a very stimulating medium for illustration. The images will always be reflective of their time, as they are constructed by deconstructing and rearranging recent mass-media photographic imagery."

United Kingdom | Illustrator

Camilla has been working as a fashion illustrator and teacher of the subject since she graduated in fashion design from Central St. Martins College of Art and Design in London in 1993. Before her success of designing a life-size mannequin of her collage girl in 2000, she has been working on line, paint and collage images for fashion editorial, pop promotion and celebrity portraits for Kylie Minogue.

CECILIA CARLSTEDT

"I have always been drawing with pencil, and that has become a sort of base for my work through developing and experimenting with other media. In the end, I really like the mixture and contrast of traditional media like pencil and ink in combination with more modern tools like vector graphics."

Sweden | Illustrator

Born in Stockholm in 1977. Based in New York City. After graduating with a Bachelor of Arts from the Graphic Design Foundation course at London College of Communication, Cecilia returned to Stockholm and worked full-time as an illustrator. Her interest in exploring the balance between design and drawing has led to a unique style which is intuitive, experimental and essentially linked to the world of fashion.

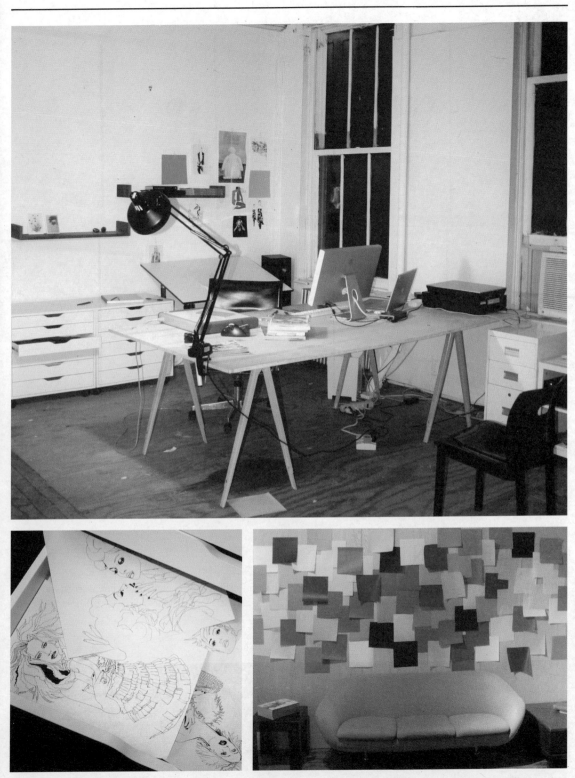

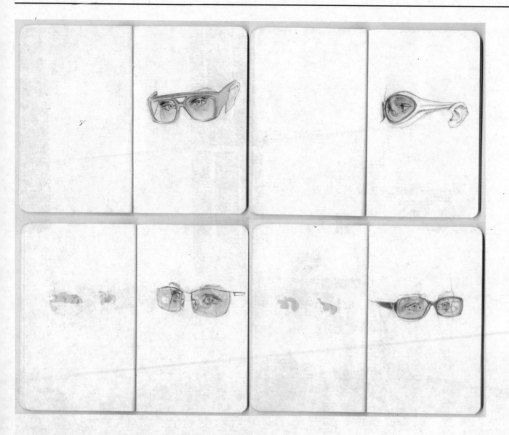

CÉDRIC RIVRAIN

"Most important to me in my work is being spontaneous, following my own instinct, never going too far, but never considering it done before I am convinced that it is. My favorite color is skin color because it is sensual and so delicate. And I love to draw with makeup because it gives an intense, deep, yet so light and shy effect."

France | Illustrator

Cédric started to learn drawing with live models in Paris, where he developed a strong sense of fashion. He has collaborated with designers such as John Galliano of Christian Dior. After his illustration for the designer Yazbukey was first published in 2000, he began contributing fashion stories for magazines such as Numéro and Tokion, as well as illustrations for Maria Luisa. His work has been exhibited in Paris, Amsterdam and Berlin.

My occupation before was fashion designer that I still keep on being aside.

My atelier and "baby baby", solo exhibition 2008 at ROCKET in Tokyo. I made macron tower, knit work, many paintings. (photo by Yoshitugu Enomoto)

CHINATSU HIGASHI

"My favorite colors are pink and green. Pink especially attracts me, with so many varieties: baby pink, salmon pink, rose pink, shocking pink... Pink reminds me of milk and blood. It's a symbol of maternal love and innocence and power. I like the contrast between baby pink and peppermint green."

Japan | Illustrator

Born in Japan in 1979. Chinatsu Higashi graduated from Nihon University College of Art and has been a freelance illustrator since 2005. She has always loved painting, drawing, collage and embroidery, using a wide range of materials, from watercolor and acrylic color to vintage cabochon button, lace, wool string, etc. By mending pieces together, she hopes to bring the past and present together for a charming and gentle impression.

CHRISTINA K.

"I create a collage and color palette in my mind or on paper that I am keen on, I meticulously draw by hand all the elements that I would like to include, and then recompose them digitally and retouch them wherever and whenever needed. I seem to always add things on a later date, leaving the artwork aside for a few days in order to see it with 'fresh eyes.'"

United Kingdom | Illustrator

Born in Athens, based in London. Christina works with both traditional and digital mark-making techniques to create delicate, ethereal illustrations. Her work has been exhibited internationally and is on permanent exhibition at Cosh Gallery in London. It has also been featured in Fashion Wonderland, Illusive 2, All Allure, Curvy Books. Her clients include Ogilvy & Mather, Levi's, Chanel, Elle, Tokion, Vogue, Esquire.

Pencil and ink are the media most dear to me. I have been trying to paint more, but I haven't yet found the best way to incorporate it into my work, as transferring painting to digital loses the depth of the original artwork. So a lot of it is just sitting in my drawers or on my walls. But any combination of pale and fluorescent colors can break my heart.

COCO PIT

"'feminine' in my eyes is an abstract construct. At the end of the day, it lies in the eye of the beholder. I tend to start my work by experimenting with old-school processes such as painting, drawing and ceramics, before designing the final image digitally. I like to mix several techniques but aim for restraint and minimalism in the finished work, as I like the results achieved from combining these two approaches."

United Kingdom | Illustrator

After studying fine arts in Paris, Coco moved to London in 2004 and set up her own company, GetConfused. She began doing illustrations for lookbooks, magazines and websites, and now creates imagery for publications spanning both the independent and mainstream press. She has also produced a collection of scarves, Forget-me-not, which is available online and in shops around the world.

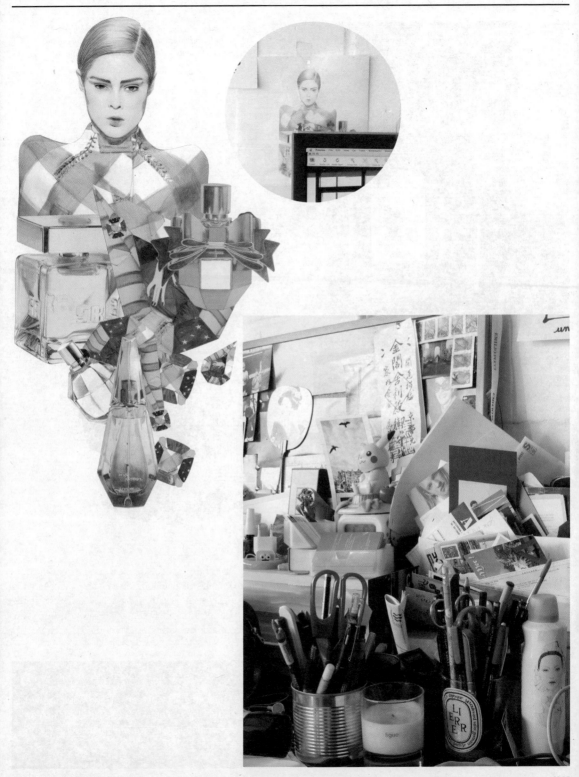

DAVID DESPAU

"I like to draw faces with simple techniques using pencil, ballpen, ink. I try to emphasize a point of interest and then dilute the rest so as to create a beautiful, harmonious composition. I love composing the illustration with typography. I always finish the illustration on the computer. I liked this style of drawing when I was studying fine arts, but I only started to develop it two years ago, because I like the faces, classic techniques (pencil, ballpen, etc) and tendencies in design and art direction."

Spain | Illustrator & Art Director

Based in Madrid, Spain. Initially an architecture student, David chose to study Fine Arts instead. After graduating with a degree in design, he continued to work in design, advertising and illustration. He has been a freelance illustrator, art director and creative director at online agencies such as Teknoland, Carat, Zapping-interactive, and Publicis. His clients include Renault, BMW, Telefónica, Beam Global, Cocacola Light, Vodafone.

I am highly influenced by Edouard Manet. I love the way his paintings commented on a bourgeois lifestyle. In terms of technique I am drawn to his manipulation of space.

ELISA JOHNS

"I pull together images from fashion magazines, photos I've taken on trips, historical painting references, and begin to build a narrative and setting around certain characters. Once the painting is planned, I focus on the types of painting surfaces I'm creating. I also focus on the atmosphere developed by the color palette."

United States | Painter

Elisa's work is a culmination of things that both attract and repulse her, focusing on the glamorous, the natural, and the absurd. Always interested in figurative painting, Elisa's style derives from the illusive quality she saw in the photographs she worked from — a fantasy where bourgeois lifestyle collides with raw nature. Beautiful people, animals and architecture are set in a lushly painted landscape.

FIFI LAPIN

"Sometimes I will start with an idea, possibly developed from my sketchbooks, and sometimes I will work organically, almost doodling my thoughts down until I am happy with the resulting image. I use simple tools to make my marks. Sometimes I leave the drawing as it is, and sometimes I may add more color digitally. I tend not to manipulate the image using the computer too much, in order to stay true to the original drawing."

United Kingdom | Illustrator

Fifi Lapin appears as the world's most stylish bunny on her blog, which features drawings of a bunny dressed in high fashion. In some cases the drawing merely displays the clothes, highlighting Fifi's fickle nature and constant need for attention; other times the drawing conveys an emotion, possibly expressing her struggle for real life. Deeply influenced by Coco Chanel, Fifi believes simplicity is the keynote of all true elegance.

GÉRALDINE GEORGES

"My work is a mix of collage, drawing and computer. Once I've finished my collage, I scan it and I clean it up. If needed, I add some details or colors. My favorite color and drawing media are black and notebooks, because I like ... For inspiration, I look at life more closely."

Belgium | Illustrator

After graduating from the Brussels Royal Academy of Fine Arts, Géraldine worked in advertising in Belgium for seven years. But since discovering her interest for photo-retouching in 2006, she has worked as a freelance illustrator. Using a variety of techniques, she creates collages of images with a feminine influence that are organic in form, giving her works a mesmerizing style that borders on the mystical.

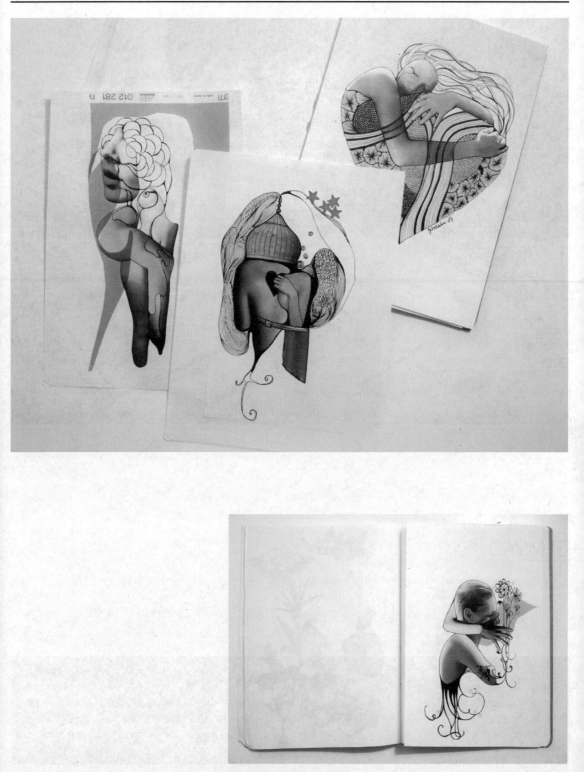

GI MYAO

"I just like to draw people with cool outfits with different media. Now, I have found a media that fits my style. I draw mostly with acrylic, it has that fresh finish and texture on paper. I usually write little notes in my sketchbook, then begin to combine different research together, to see what looks best. I will not draw the final piece until I'm totally satisfied."

United Kingdom | Illustrator

Based in London. Gi Myao began drawing at the age of four, and spent 12 years in different art schools before she was admitted to Central Saint Martins in London. After graduating with a Bachelor of Arts majoring in fashion design in 2006, Myao joined The Anna Su Agency. Since then her works have received several awards, including the London Institute's Nina De York Illustration Award.

Vivienne Westwood spring/summer 2009
18 Jan 2009

HELENE RYENBAKKEN

"My drawings are usually ugly, vulgar versions of the truth. I tend to exaggerate a person's features. Not necessarily on purpose, but something subconsciously makes me draw bigger jaw lines, more defined cheek bones, lips and eyes. And they also often look like they are afflicted with arthritis."

Norway | Illustrator

Currently a final-year student majoring in graphic design at Westerdals School of Communication in Norway, Helene began her career as an illustrator a couple of years ago, working mainly for Norwegian magazines. Her personal artwork is most often about the female, emphasizing makeup or a feminine posture, with subconsciously exaggerated facial traits.

IZUMI IDOIA ZUBIA

"I like to think about projects while I'm walking, then stop for a coffee and quickly draw the ideas that come to me in my sketchbook. Then I go home and concentrate on the drawings and paintings for hours, while listening to music that helps me enter deep into my world. When I have made everything that I need, I scan them and finalize on the computer. Sometimes I add some textures in Photoshop or Illustrator."

France | Illustrator

Based in Paris. After graduating with degrees in architecture, multimedia arts and lyrical music, Izumi worked in Barcelona as a web/graphic designer and illustrator before returning to Paris to work as a freelance illustrator in 2006. Specialized in fashion illustration, textile prints, flash animations and children's books and magazines, her clients include Balenciaga, Boba-Gimenez & Zuazo, Editions Milan, Mon Petit Art and Artifiz.

"Feminine" in my eyes are eyes, clouds, mountains, sea, flowers, earth, cats, asia, dancers, singers, poetry, cello, chocolate…

For inspiraton I watch a lot of films, music videos, animations and images, as well as going out and about in East London to see what is happening on the streets!

JAMES HAMILTON BUTLER

"I usually get an idea in my head, then begin a process of sketching and conceptualizing. Depending on the job (personal or professional) the work will undergo a variety of changes and revisions before finalizing itself in some form or other. Sometimes, however, my first idea can be just right, as it seems to be my immediate response to a stimulus or challenge — I enjoy the spontaneity of those moments!"

Japan | Illustrator

Fashion-oriented, James has illustrated for fashion, costume, embroidery design, illustrative and print-based garment collections. In addition to print works and exhibitions, he has formed creative partnerships in photography, styling, graphics and illustration for editorial. His clients include Swarovski, PUMA, Coppernob, BLOW pr and Firetrap. Recently he is exploring 3D strategies and pattern/optical focuses.

JAMES JEAN

"I've always been interested in creating elegant compositions – the lines and proportions that I play with exploit a sensual spectrum of drawing. I usually start with a lot of rough sketching, erasing and adjusting the drawing until it crystallizes into something concrete. I do a lot of research online and in my library. It's amazing to see the depth of visual culture that humans have created through the centuries."

United States | Illustrator

Born in Taiwan and raised in New Jersey, now based in Los Angeles. He graduated from the New York School of Visual Arts in 2001. In addition to cover art for DC Comics, Jean has produced work for The New York Times, Wired, Rolling Stone, Nike and Prada. Since 2007, he has focused exclusively on personal paintings, book projects and gallery shows. In 2009, he held a solo exhibition in Kindling, Jonathan Lavine Gallery in New York City.

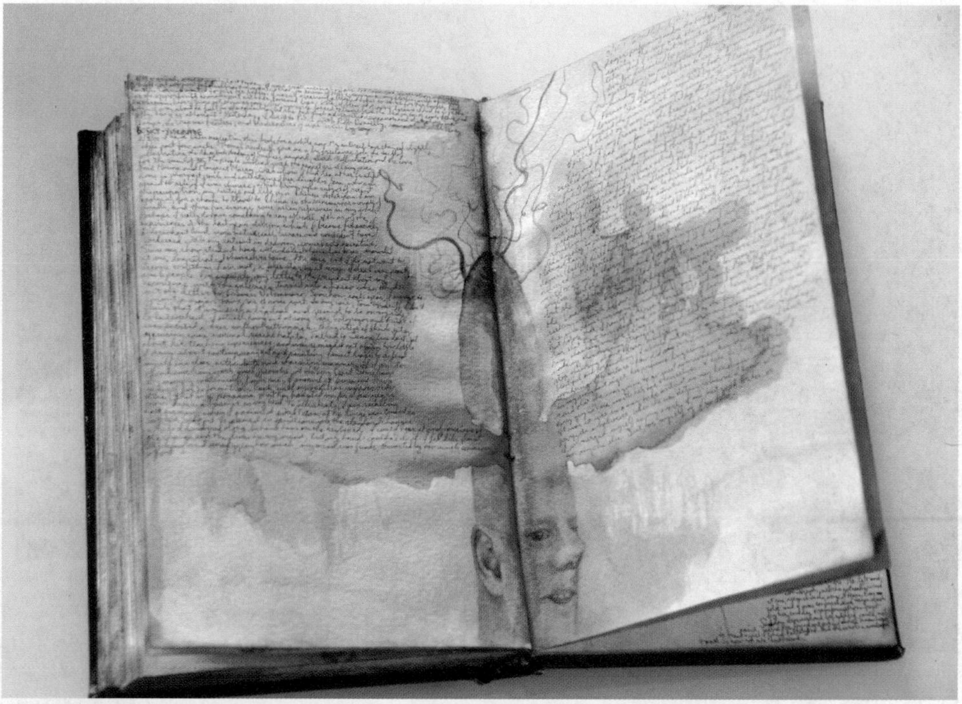

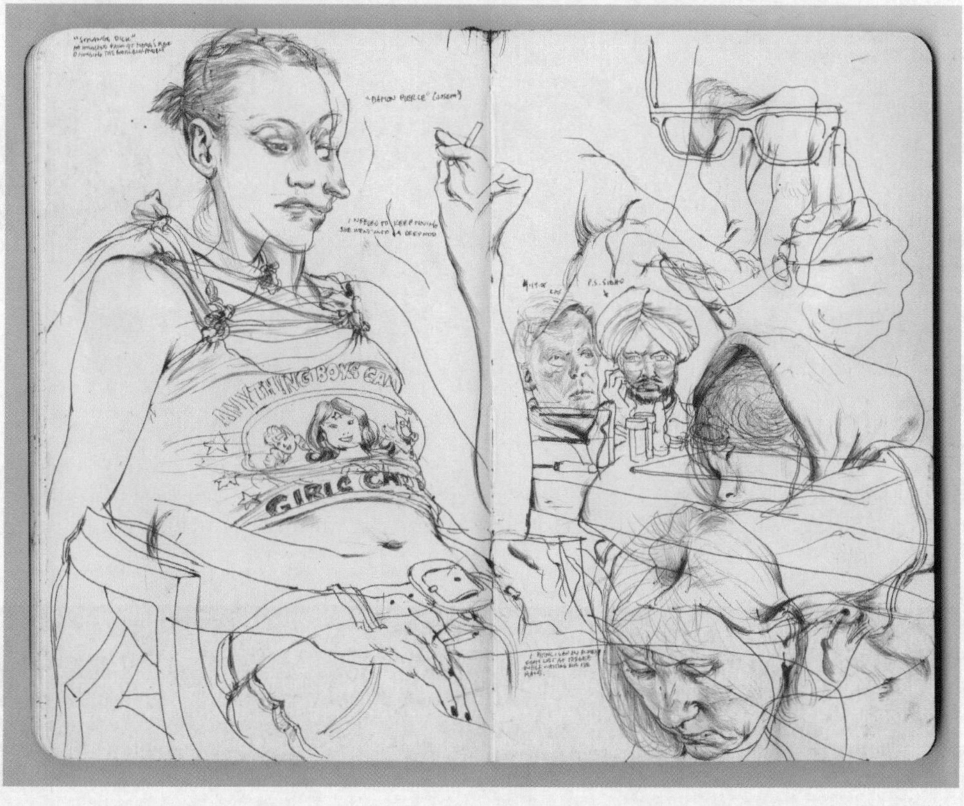

JARNO KETTUNEN

"I usually draw very directly. I work with live models or by using photos as a reference. Most of the time goes to selecting the techniques and materials. Then I draw until I get one drawing that I like. After that I scan the drawing and maybe alter it or clean it up with Photoshop."

Belgium | Illustrator

This young Finnish illustrator is dedicated to high fashion, lifestyles and luxury, inspired by the traditional techniques of fine art. His illustrations began to draw attention in the world fashion industry when he was asked to perform live drawing in the backstage of the Wendy & Jim Homme fashion show in Paris in 2007.

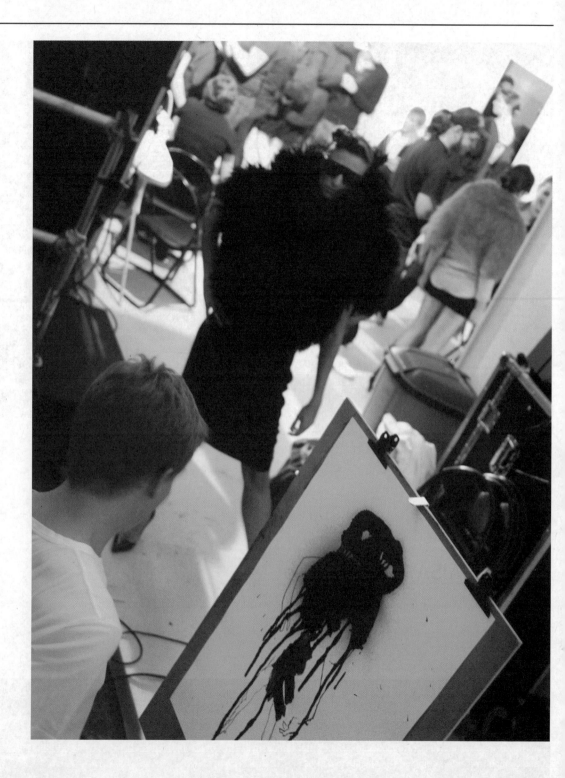

I love collage since I was a child, I used to cut and paste pictures that I offered to my parents. I've always kept magazines, photographs and colored papers...

KARINE DAISAY

"I begin by drawing; I'm looking for a composition, an idea. Once the design is finished, I look in my archive: papers, photos, head for the characters. Finally I start to stick a colored background, it gives me the tone, the atmosphere of the image. My scissors in hand, I cut, glue and assemble... I love that technology is the background, that there is more atmosphere than the collage."

France | Illustrator

Born in Rennes, France, in 1971. Based in Paris. Karine studied in Paris before attending the Beaux Arts of Rennes, where she graduated in 1996. She loved making collages as a child, and today her mixed-media illustrations are unique in the world of fashion illustration. With the belief that feminism is a mix of strength and softness, she mixes illustration and collage to create a colorful, stylish and bold style.

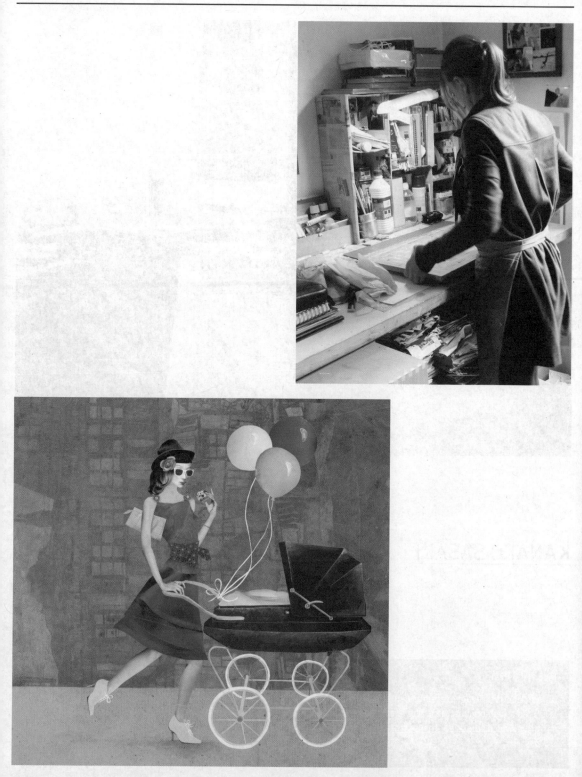

KANAKO SASAKI

"For me the creative process begins as I draw in my mind – a new image often flashes before me when I'm in a state between sleeping and waking (but not suffering from lack of sleep). For inspiration, I go outside and see, or hear, scenery, colors, patterns, people and sounds."

Japan | Illustrator

Born in Sendai, Miyagi prefecture, in 1983. Graduated from Tohoku Institute of Technology, before moving to Tokyo in 2005. As a fashion illustrator, she is attracted to the flow and bleed of watercolors. Her creative process begins with a narrative, which guides her to illustrate the whole story in a single drawing.

KITTOZUTTO

"Our work process consists of: forming up a rough idea; finding image references and piecing them together as a guide; rough sketch; adjustments; detailed illustration; coloring; adding of details. We prefer to go digital because it's less messy. 'Feminine' in my eyes is Curls, Swirls, female and watercolors."

Malaysia and Singapore | Art and design boutique

Kittozutto is an art and design boutique comprising the design duo, Yana Ee from Malaysia and Teo Wei Jun from Singapore, who met while working at Oglivy Singapore. Their hyperrealistic yet surreal illustrations are inspired by women, fluids and nature, combining fine art illustrations with digital imaging techniques to create extremely detailed artworks.

LAURA LAINE

"I feel that my drawing is a somewhat spontaneous action, I'm not so conscious about style. I love black and white using pencil, ink and markers. I prefer black and white because I feel like I can best express what I want with lines and surfaces, and color would often only interfere with that and be a distraction. I like to maintain a certain sense of purity in my drawings through using black -and-white technique."

Finland | Illustrator

Based in Helsinki. Laura studied fashion design at University of Art and Design Helsinki, where she is currently teaching fashion illustration. Her precise drawing comes from the fine pencil-tip, which draws the melancholy flounce and fancy style of her twisted-bodied girls. Her clients include T magazine, the Guardian, Marimekko, Vive la Mode magazine, Wunder and Daniel Palillo.

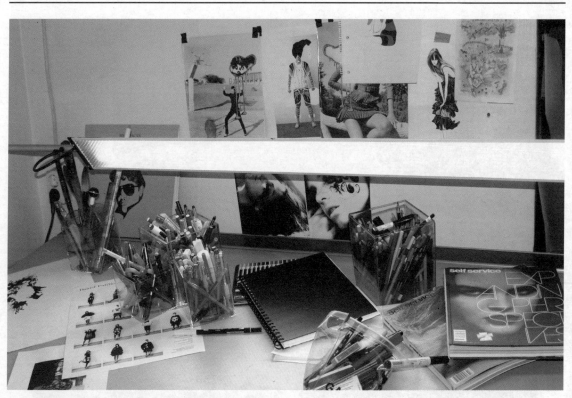

I start with an idea of what feeling and movement I want the end result to have, and then as I draw the idea develops and gets more defined. I draw with pencil and markers and finally retouch the image in Photoshop.

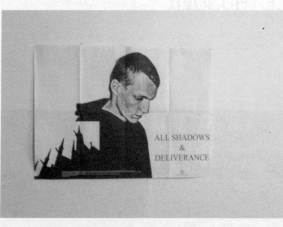

LITTLE THUNDER

"Inspiration comes to me most often when I'm taking a bath or before I go to sleep. I'm very much influenced by the American comic artist Chris Ware. His comic stories always make me cry."

Hong Kong | Comic artist & illustrator

Born in Hong Kong in 1984, Little Thunder published her first artwork in a comic magazine at age 11. Since then she has diligently pursued her craft, publishing her first book in Hong Kong in July 2009. She also collaborates with the Belgian comic publisher Dargaud, while her full-color comic series "Kylooe" is published in France.

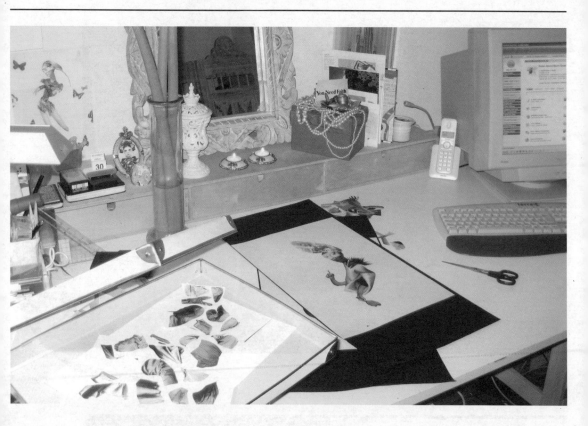

MAREN ESDAR

"Using collage-technique in the field of fashion was something experimental to me. I was searching for a possibility to create something new, something which hasn't been seen before (at least I hadn't), something 'unique'. I'm used to the technique of collage since high school. Somehow it appeared to be a natural move to experiment with it."

Germany | Illustrator

Born in Westphalia, Germany, in 1972. Based in Hamburg. Maren was educated both as a stylist and illustrator at the University of Applied Sciences in Hamburg and Central St. Martins in London. Her extravagant, surreal and stylish collages have been featured in Vogue, New York Times Magazine, "Fashion Illustration Next", "Wonderland", "illusive 1+2" and "Fashion Unfolding".

Developing and finishing a drawing is always a kind of "fight". I need to focus before getting started, which is not always easy, especially if I feel more like going out and having fun. Once I finally get started, I struggle with myself to get to an end, because I'm hardly ever satisfied, always finding something to improve. Only the deadline forces me to finish by defining the end.

MIYUKI OHASHI

"Sometimes I do sketches, but generally I draw directly on the rough layout. I love all colors, but if I must choose, I would say black and white. I love the texture that black pencil lines draw on white paper. My favorite drawing media are pencils and acrylic paints, so familiar to me, as I am used to drawing with them."

Japan | Illustrator

Born in Tochigi, Japan. After graduating from Saitama's Dokkyo University with a degree in French, she enrolled in Setsu Mode Seminar in Tokyo. Her first exhibition "Miyuki-Miyuki" was held at Morgan Café in 1999. Since 2001, her drawings appear in department store advertisements, magazines, books and greeting cards. Her solo exhibition "Miyuki Ohashi Illustration, Currently" was held at Gekkoso in Ginza, Tokyo, in 2007.

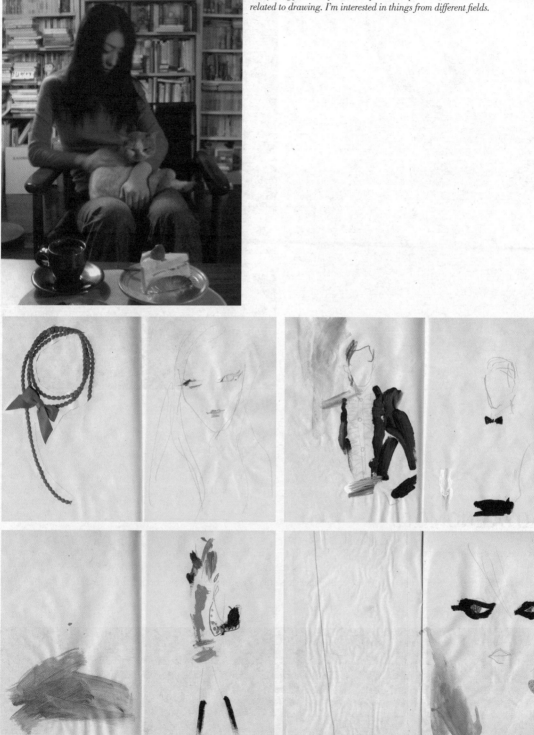

Everything from the past to the present inspires me, whether or not it is directly related to drawing. I'm interested in things from different fields.

NAOYA ENOMOTO

"I would describe my work as beautiful, fresh, and a bit surprising. I get inspiration from seeing, feeling and touching everything around me that I find interesting. I start by developing visual ideas in my head. Then I draw them on paper, scan what I've drawn into my Mac, and work on it until I get it done. I see 'feminine' as something delicate. Its color would be either purple or pink."

Japan | Designer

Born in Japan in 1980. Naoya Enomoto has been working as a graphic and editorial designer since he graduated from design studies at Tokyo Polytechnic University. His works are drawn with fine, curvy lines and a soft, feminine touch. His illustrations and artworks have appeared in magazines and books, including STU MAGAZINE No.28, rtr. Magazine, onthecamper_compendium, and iLLUSTRATiON BOOK PRO 02.

I'm working on graphic design most of the time, so I don't have much time for socializing.

NAJA CONRAD-HANSEN

"I start with a sentence in my mind and go from there. I like to think a nice artwork is like telling stories in pictures, stories that can change depending of the eye of the beholder. Feminine for me is many things, but first is the details in a work and a great eye for color. Many more men than women are color-blind."

Denmark | Artist & designer

After graduating from Denmark Design School, Naja began a career as an artist and designer in 2003. Her work embraces illustration, painting, graphic design, fashion concepts and silk-screen prints, appearing in fashion/graphic magazines and books. She also designs prints and patterns for clothing labels and in limited editions for her own brand Meannorth. She was one of "200 best illustrators worldwide" 2007/08, by Lürzer's Archive.

NADIA FLOWER

"Pastel colors are important in my work for expressing femininity, along with soft pencil lines, and intricate details and texture. I guess for me it's more of a feeling one conveys. And my favorite media would be watercolor and pencil. I love watercolor, as the fluidity can create such delicate, dream-like effects."

New Zealand | Illustrator

Nadia's work has appeared in group exhibitions and book publications in Australia, Japan and the US. Her illustrations are playful and sensual, where fantasies and fashion collide. Combining hand-drawn and computer-based imagery, Nadia works across a variety of visual media, from fine-art painting to fashion and textile, as well as pure illustration for the editorial and advertising markets.

When I think of "feminine", straight away I think of beautiful dresses and color.

PAULA SANZ CABALLERO

"I started 10 years ago, on a long flight to Toronto. I had no book to read, no pencil to draw, but I had a piece of fabric and a hotel sewing kit. I enjoyed it so much and the flight seemed so short in time to me, that I thought I had found an interesting way of expressing my world. Feminine to me means silence, mystery, discreet elegance and an attitude of being close and distant at the same time."

Spain | Painter

Based in Valencia. After graduating with a Bachelor of Arts in Fine Arts from the University of Valencia, Paula started her career as a painter, and in the late 1990s began experimenting with textiles and embroidery, which eventually became the chosen medium for her visual narratives. As a fabric artist, her clients include Ann Taylor Loft and Roger La Borde, as well as international fashion and design magazines.

There's no process established for me. Some days I just need my mind, pencil, paper and one minute to do it. Other times, I need a lot of time, extra inspiration from pictures and patience.

After I got my first aquarelle, I experimented with that color technique and found new prospects for my working process. In this way I developed my individual style.

PETRA DUFKOVA

"My work is the achievement of a long research, a composition of a lot of ideas and inspirations. I'm very interested in fashion, so my drawings are essentially figurative themes, for example fashion design or impression, but I make graphic works, prints and color-intensive paintings and textile paintings too."

Czech Republic | Illustrator, stylist & fashion designer

Born in Uherske Hradiste, Czech Republic. Petra graduated from the international fashion school Esmod in Munich in 2008, with a prêt-a-porter collection. Ever since she won the Best Illustration Award in 2008 with her collection at the China Fashion Week, Petra has been working as a freelance illustrator, stylist and fashion designer.

RAPHAËL VICENZI

"It has to start with an idea, usually a short sentence associated with some intellectual or emotional perspective. Sometimes the illustration is fully formed in my head before I start. Sometimes it turns into something unexpected in mid-course. I draw the lines and doodles in Photoshop or Illustrator, make new watercolors on cheap A4 paper, use my 2-year-old's blue bic drawings, browse through my scan collection and build the whole illustration from there."

Belgium | Illustrator

Born in 1972 in Charleroi, Belgium. Based in Brussels. Also known as My Dead Pony, Raphaël Vicenzi is a self-taught illustrator, whose illustrations are a combination of digital media and watercolors influenced by his many readings, interest in human nature and the world around him.

I was fed up of doing mostly vector graphics. I needed something more immediate, something that allowed me to mess things up and use watercolors, gouache, blue bic and trash things up. I was very interested in mixing watercolors with digital, but at first I didn't dare. Now that I've gained confidence, it feels natural and instinctive for me to work this way.

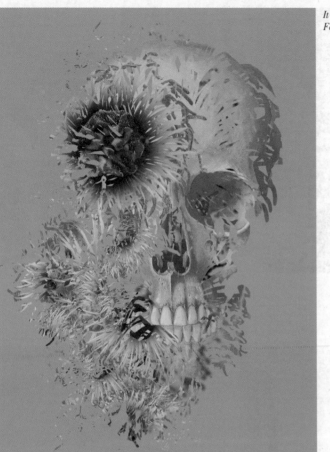

RYO SAKUMA

"The science and philosophy that explain the nature of mankind, the environment and the economy interest me, using animals and plants to produce my artwork. I like black and white. And I like to use Photoshop to draw, because it contains everything, as it doesn't contain anything. Inspiration comes from nature, humankind, art, design, music, movies, etc."

Japan | Graphic designer

Born in Hokkaido, Japan, in 1982. Now based in Saitama. Ryo graduated with a university degree in economics, but has been working as a freelance graphic artist and designer since 2008. Inspired by human immortality, his drawings illustrate his philosophy on the relationship between human nature and the environment.

MAT MAITLAND

"My final pieces are always a work in progress. I do no sketches or roughs. As soon as I start an image, it is the final piece, meaning that I work on it until I am happy. So it is a decision-making process, an exciting and unexpected journey with random picture choices taking me to the final destination."

Japan | Illustrator

Mat began his graphic design career by designing record covers at Warner Brothers Records. As a teenager, he was deeply influenced by Andy Warhol. Realizing that art didn't have to be purely craft-based, Mat evolved into an image-maker with a solid understanding of pop culture. From bright glossy magazine colors to lips or cut-out eyes, these elements in his works are juxtaposed to create energetic, bold compositions.

I love all colors, it's hard to pick one! I guess my favorite drawing media would be a mouse and Photoshop.

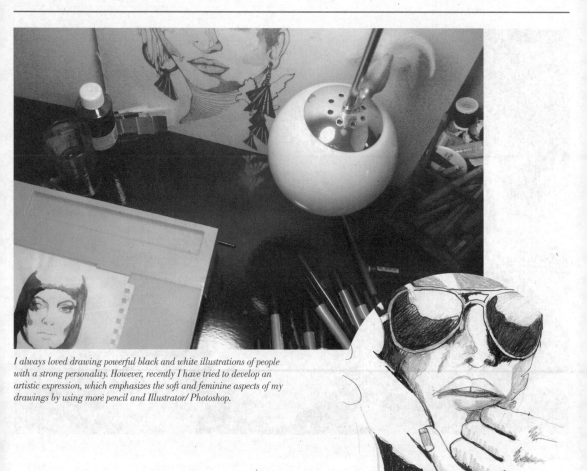

I always loved drawing powerful black and white illustrations of people with a strong personality. However, recently I have tried to develop an artistic expression, which emphasizes the soft and feminine aspects of my drawings by using more pencil and Illustrator/Photoshop.

TENNA HANSEN

"I like to use both pencil and ink in my illustrations, because the two media unify the feminine and masculine aspects in my drawings. I get an idea, analyze the theme, choose a style that matches the theme, choose the right combination of drawing media, draw the illustration and finish it in Illustrator or Photoshop. I often put a lot of effort into the analysis of the theme. Thereafter, it is a question of exploring the different possibilities."

Denmark | Illustrator, graphic designer

Born in 1977. Based in Copenhagen. Since graduating from the Danish Design School with a degree in fashion, her passion has driven her toward a career as an illustrator. In 2005 she started her own company producing illustrations, print and graphic designs. Using pencils and ink, her trademark works of sensual feminine expression have been published in books and fashion magazines around the world.

In the beginning, my mode of expression seemed to be oil painting thickly applied to the canvas with acrylic paint. But my style changed when I encountered the work of Susan Cianciolo at her exhibition in Shibuya, Tokyo. My heart was struck by her free mode of expression and technique.

TOSHIMITSU HARUKA

"My favorite color is fluorescent pink, as an image of neon signs at night, which feels erotically feminine. My favorite drawing media are acrylic paint, color pencil, titanium pencil and Photoshop (although the PC is used only to arrange a layout). The reason I adhere to hand-drawn is that a line can express my feeling directly."

Japan | Illustrator

Born in 1983. After graduating from Toyo Institute of Art & Design, Toshimitsu Haruka began her career as a fashion illustrator. She participated in "MULTIPLE MARMELADE 2005 Spring/Summer COLLECTION" of Tokyo Collection, producing life-sized corrugated cardboard mannequins instead of fashion models.

WENDY PLOVMAND

"With commercial work, I receive a brief and work around the concept, while drawing and playing with the work during the process. I like that my final artwork surprises me and hate to do 'copies' of my old work. When clients refer to an older project I've done, I always try to do something slightly different and new. My art projects are often based on an idea that I've had in mind a longer time, and I approach it with sketches, words, photos until I'm ready to execute it in whatever media it craves!"

Denmark | Illustrator

Born and based in Copenhagen. Wendy has been working as a professional artist and illustrator since graduating from the Danish Design School in 2001. She has earned grants from national institutions, while her works have been exhibited in Copenhagen, Berlin and London, and published in numerous international books and publications from Mexico to Japan, by Taschen, Die Gestalten, Victionary, Images 32, etc.

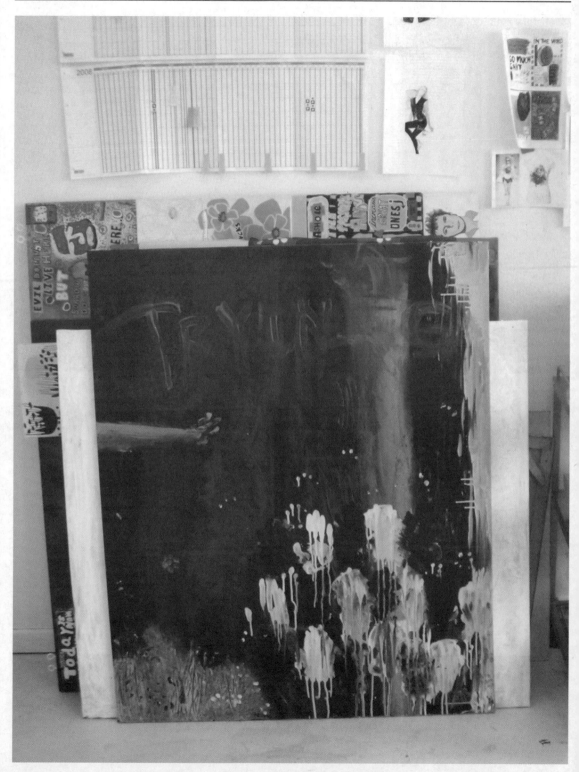

YOSHI TAJIMA

"My work is a balance between confusion and order, which mixes parts of face, body and fantasy. My favorite color is purple, because it is sensuous. My favorite drawing medium is pencil, because it is sensitive. I get inspiration from reading, cycling and clubbing."

Japan | Graphic designer & illustrator

Based in Tokyo. Loves cats, curry and dance music. Founded the design agency RADIO in 1998 and has been contributing graphic art and illustrations to magazines and publications since 2004. He is a member of Mirage, an experimental graphic-art partnership with Toshifumi Tanabu and Takeshi Tonemochi. Yoshi's first picture book "Paris! Cirque! Paris!" was published in 2007.

YOKO HASEGAWA

"I love antique materials, especially antique laces and kimono fabrics, which I have been collecting for several years. I was familiar with collage techniques since university. I love delicate shades of light purples, which involve contradictory images of elegant, pure, erotic. It is challenging to use the same color and draw illustrations with completely different images."

Japan | Illustrator

Born in 1981. Yoko graduated in design from Tama Art University and worked for an apparel company before working as a freelance illustrator since 2006. For her collages, she collects antique materials from around the world, such as laces, kimono fabrics, beads and old paper items. Her work includes illustrations for fashion magazines, CD jackets, book covers and packaging. She held a solo exhibition at Tray Gallery in Tokyo in 2008.

ZAXIIV

"My favorite color is black and white. Because black can't dye and white can dye. This looks like my personality. For me feminine means no colors, transparency. To develop a drawing, I imagine for a long time, and then I draw. I am inspired by everything that falls under my gaze."

Japan | Graphic design

ZAXIIV is a design studio established by Japan-based graphic designer Keita Oguchi in 2007. They do graphic design and illustrations for apparel brands such as And A and MACARONIC, as well as magazines such as MdN, and music production design. They also work on their own solo exhibitions.

Creative & Editorial Direction
AllRightsReserved Publishing

Art Direction & Design
Yan@AllRightsReserved Ltd.

Copywriter
Cherise Fong

Editorial Assistant
Ashley Chan@AllRightsReserved Ltd.

First Published in 2010 by AllRightsReserved Ltd.
tel: (852) 27120873
fax: (852) 27126701
website: www.allrights-reserved.com

For General Enquiry: info@allrights-reserved.com
For Distribution: books@allrights-reserved.com
For Editorial Submission & Collaborations:
editor@allrights-reserved.com

Find us on Facebook:
Please search "AllRightsReserved"

Published in Hong Kong
ISBN 978-988-17971-1-7

Roses

English